THE
TOTALLY EGGS
COOKBOOK

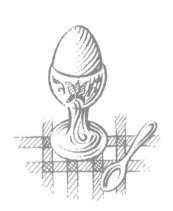

THE TOTALLY EGGS COOKBOOK

by Helene Siegel

Illustrated by Caroline Vibbert

CELESTIAL ARTS
BERKELEY, CALIFORNIA

The Totally Eggs Cookbook is produced by becker&mayer!, Ltd.

Printed in Singapore.

Cover design and illustration: Bob Greisen
Interior design and typesetting: Susan Hernday
Interior illustrations: Carolyn Vibbert

Library of Congress Cataloging-in-Publication Data
Siegel, Helene.
    The Totally Eggs Cookbook / by Helene Siegel.
        p.   cm.
    ISBN-13: 978-0-89087-833-0 / ISBN-10: 0-89087-833-1
    1. Cookery (Eggs)   I. Title.
TX745.S54   1997
641.6'75—dc21   97-20154
                                                      CIP

Celestial Arts Publishing
P.O. Box 7123
Berkeley, CA 94707

Look for other books in the *Totally* series at your local store!

FOR ANDREW, WHO IS ALWAYS READY TO EAT AN EGG.

CONTENTS

INTRODUCTION

I have never given up on the egg. How could I?

They are as indispensable to good cooking as salt and pepper. Without eggs in the kitchen, puddings and flans would flounder; the glorious French sauces like mayonnaise and hollandaise would vanish; rich, silky ice creams would give way to thin ice milks and sorbets; cakes and tortes would be pale imitations of themselves; and the soufflé would cease to rise.

And that is just scratching the surface.

Eggs also play a very special role in our ability to care for ourselves and feed others. They are always available at a low price at the supermarket, and they keep in the refrigerator for weeks. Even a child (or a confirmed noncook) can be taught to scramble or boil an egg if the cook is not at home. The mild richness and high nutritional value of eggs make them ideal for those recuperating from illness or childbirth, and for those who simply want something comforting to eat—quickly.

Now that the dust is settling on the great egg and cholesterol scare of the last twenty years, opinions about the consumption of eggs seem to be finding a more sensible middle ground. Eggs are now sanctioned by the American Heart Association, for those without already elevated blood cholesterol levels, at the rate of about four a week.

So dig in. The eggs are lovely.

"Where is it written in stone that we always have to be served two eggs cooked the same way?"
    —*from* The Breakfast Book *by*
    Marion Cunningham

BREAKFAST BABIES

SCRAMBLED EGGS
WITH CHEESE

How you like your morning eggs is definitely a personal matter, so take this recipe with a grain of salt. (For the slow-cooked French method, see page 30, "Scrambled Eggs and Caviar.")

2 eggs
2 tablespoons milk
salt and freshly ground pepper
2 or 3 dashes Tabasco
2 teaspoons butter
¼ cup grated cheddar cheese *or* 1 ounce
    cream cheese

In a bowl, beat together eggs, milk, salt, pepper, and Tabasco with a fork.

Melt the butter in a small skillet over medium-high heat. Pour in the eggs, swirl the pan, reduce heat to medium, and cook—flipping, turning, and otherwise scrambling—until nearly done. Sprinkle in grated cheese or crumbled cream cheese, scramble once or twice to melt, and serve.

SERVES 1

"There is always a best way of doing everything, if it be to boil an egg."
        —Ralph Waldo Emerson

SOFT-BOILED EGGS
WITH TOAST FINGERS

To me soft-boiling is perfect for tender tummies or on the day after an indulgent evening. If you own an eggcup, so much the better!

eggs
water
salt and freshly ground pepper
sliced bread for toasting
butter

Place refrigerated eggs in saucepan and cover generously with cold water. Bring to a boil over medium heat. Reduce to a simmer and cook 2 to 4 minutes to taste. Remove with slotted spoon. Serve in eggcup, or crack and spoon into serving bowls. Serve with salt and pepper.

Meanwhile toast bread, and spread with butter. Cut into ½-inch-wide strips or "fingers" for dipping into yolks.

TOAD IN THE HOLE

Conceptually cute foods such as this have a place in everyone's diet. Why else do we eat, but to feel good?

1 bread slice
1 tablespoon butter
1 egg
salt and freshly ground pepper

Lightly toast the bread. With a 2-inch-round cookie cutter or small drinking glass, cut out a hole in the center.

Melt the butter in a small skillet over medium-low heat. Add the bread to the pan. Crack the egg, and empty into hole, with yolk in center and white overflowing bread. Reduce heat to low, cover, and cook until egg is done to taste, 1 to 2 minutes. Transfer with spatula to plate, and serve with salt and pepper.

SERVES 1

BAKED EGGS WITH PARMESAN AND BASIL

Oven-baked single servings, also known as en cocotte or shirred, are an excellent choice for serving eggs to a group.

olive oil for coating
4 teaspoons chopped fresh basil
4 eggs
8 teaspoons grated Parmesan cheese
freshly ground pepper

Preheat oven to 400 degrees F. Lightly coat four 4-ounce ramekins with olive oil, and place in roasting pan. Bring a pot of water to a boil.

Sprinkle basil on the bottom of each ramekin. Crack one egg at a time, and place each in a cup over the basil. Sprinkle 2 teaspoons of Parmesan over each. Pour hot water into pan until it rises halfway up sides of ramekins.

Bake about 10 minutes, until yolks are just set. Sprinkle with pepper, and serve with crusty Italian bread.

SERVES 4

Freshness of Eggs

Before modern refrigeration and distribution, an uncooked egg was always suspect of being past its prime. Nowadays, with proper refrigeration, eggs can keep as long as three weeks once you bring them home. One test for freshness is that an egg should feel heavy in the hand. If you crack it open on a plate, the yolk should stand up high in the center and the whites should form a neat circle and not be too runny. Another method for testing freshness is to place an uncracked egg in a bowl of water: An egg that floats is too old—a sinker is fresh.

HOME EGG MUFFIN SANDWICH

Here is what I make when my son has a craving for breakfast at a certain drive-through hamburger stand. Use a biscuit or cookie cutter to cut the ham, and substitute poached or fried eggs as you choose.

1 English muffin
butter for coating
cheddar cheese slices
1 tablespoon butter
1 3-inch round, ¼-inch-thick slice
    honey-cured ham *or* Canadian bacon
1 egg beaten with Tabasco and salt
    to taste

Split and lightly toast the muffin. Butter the muffin slices and cover each with cheese. Return to toaster if using toaster oven, and brown to melt cheese. Or place slices under a hot broiler just long enough to melt cheese. Transfer to plate.

Melt the butter in a small skillet over low heat. Fry the ham or bacon until edges are brown on both sides. Place on one muffin half. Turn up the heat under the skillet to high. Add the beaten egg, and quickly scramble omelet-style to form a compact round shape. Turn out onto second muffin half. Close the sandwich and serve.

MAKES 1

How to Store Eggs

Eggs should always be stored in the refrigerator, preferably on an interior shelf where it is colder than on the inside of the door. Uncracked eggs may be kept up to three weeks. An unrefrigerated egg will age more in one day than in one week in the refrigerator. Cooked eggs should also be refrigerated.

POACHED EGGS À LA MICRO

If you are passionate about perfectly poached eggs, you must try this microwave method—it is foolproof if you cook in 30-second bursts. For an alternative stovetop method, see page 32, "Hot Egg and Bacon Salad."

▓ 1 egg

Fill an ovenproof coffee cup or 4-ounce ramekin with about 2 tablespoons water. Carefully break the egg into the water. With a toothpick or skewer, prick the yolk four or five times. Loosely cover with plastic, and microwave 30 seconds to 1 minute at full power. Let rest, covered, 1 minute. Lift out with slotted spoon and serve.

SERVES 1

SPINACH AND EGG GARLIC TOASTS

A rustic peasant dish like this also makes a satisfying dinner for one.

olive oil
2½-inch-thick slices Italian country bread
2 garlic cloves, minced
3½ ounces (about 3 cups) baby spinach
salt and freshly ground pepper
2 eggs, poached

Lightly coat a medium skillet with olive oil, and place over medium heat. Fry the bread until crisp and golden on both sides. Transfer to plate.

Add 1 or 2 tablespoons of oil to the pan, and turn heat to high. Add garlic, spinach, salt, and pepper, and cook, turning frequently, until wilted, bright green, and fragrant. Cover bread with spinach. Top with eggs, and serve with salt and pepper.

SERVES 1

FRIED EGGS

Nonstick pans are always a plus for fool-proof egg turning.

2 teaspoons butter
2 eggs
salt and freshly ground pepper

Melt the butter in a small skillet over medium-high heat. Carefully crack the eggs and slide into pan. Immediately reduce heat to low, and for sunny-side up, cook until whites are just set. For over-easy eggs, carefully turn with spatula and cook an additional 5 seconds. Salt and pepper to taste.

MAKES 2

"The egg is to cuisine what the article is to speech."

—Anonymous

FRIED EGG SANDWICH

Here is a lunch counter favorite.

2 slices egg bread *or* challah *or* rye, toasted
butter for coating
tomato slices
3 slices bacon, fried and drained
4 sprigs watercress
1 egg, fried over-easy
salt and freshly ground pepper

Butter the toast. On one slice, layer the tomato and bacon. On the other slice, layer watercress and top with hot fried egg. Season to taste with salt and pepper, and close sandwich. Slice and serve.

MAKES 1

BREAKFAST BURRITOS SANS BEANS

I love Mexican food but I'm not much of a bean person first thing in the morning. These rolled tortillas contain just eggs and a healthy helping of roasted chiles.

2 flour tortillas
4 eggs
¼ cup heavy cream
salt
2 teaspoons butter
2 poblano chiles, roasted, peeled, seeded, and diced
¼ cup sour cream
chopped red onion, cilantro, tomatoes, and grated cheddar for garnish

Wrap tortillas in foil, and warm in a 350-degree F oven 10 minutes.

Lightly beat eggs with cream and salt. Melt butter in medium skillet over medium heat. Pour in eggs and poblanos. Reduce heat and cook, stirring constantly, until soft curds form.

Spread each tortilla on a counter. In its center, spread each with about 1 spoonful of sour cream. Spoon eggs on top, and garnish with onion, cilantro, tomatoes, or cheddar cheese. Fold bottom and then sides to enclose, and serve.

SERVES 2 TO 4

To substitute yolks or whites for a whole egg, use two of each for one egg.

STARTERS, SOUPS,
AND
SALADS

HARD-BOILED EGGS

Little in life is more frustrating than a hard-boiled egg that won't release its shell or a yolk that remains uncooked. Complete satisfaction is guaranteed with the following method.

Place the refrigerated eggs in a single layer in a saucepan and add enough cold tap water to cover generously. Bring to a boil, reduce to a simmer, and cook 12 minutes. Immediately drain, fill the pot with cold water, and crack the shells against the sides of the pan. Peel and chill.

Eggs that have been colored and dyed for Easter—even those that are hard-boiled—should not be eaten if they have been out of the refrigerator for more than two hours.

EGG SALAD

Here is a plain, delicious egg salad for making sandwiches, spreading on crackers, or enriching salads.

4 hard-boiled eggs, cooled and peeled
¼ cup chopped red onion
3 tablespoons prepared mayonnaise
2 tablespoons chopped fresh tarragon *or* basil
salt and freshly ground pepper

Separate the egg yolks and whites. Chop the whites and crumble the yolks. Place in a bowl with onion, mayonnaise, tarragon or basil, salt, and pepper. Lightly mix and mash with a fork, and adjust seasonings.

MAKES 2 SANDWICHES

A green ring on a hard-boiled egg yolk indicates the egg has been overcooked. It is not a safety problem.

CHUTNEY DEVILED EGGS

Here is a sweet, spicy spin on a favorite picnic food.

4 hard-boiled eggs
2 tablespoons sour cream
1 tablespoon mango chutney, chopped
¼ teaspoon curry powder
salt and Tabasco
2 scallions, trimmed and minced

Peel the eggs and cut in half lengthwise. Carefully remove the yolks and place them in a bowl. Place whites on platter, cut-side up.

Gently mash the yolks with a fork. In another small bowl, mix together sour cream, chutney, curry, salt, and Tabasco to taste. Add to yolks along with scallions, and mash into a paste. Mound into egg whites and serve, or reserve, covered, in the refrigerator.

SERVES 4

SCRAMBLED EGGS AND CAVIAR

In this luxurious French appetizer, eggs from the farm and eggs from the sea combine with finesse.

4 eggs
3 tablespoons half-and-half
salt and freshly ground pepper
2 tablespoons butter
4 tablespoons sour cream
1 ounce caviar
plain crackers *or* dry toast points
    or "fingers"

Combine eggs, half-and-half, salt, and pepper in mixing bowl, and beat.

Melt butter in large skillet over moderate heat. Pour in eggs, reduce heat to medium-low, and cook, stirring constantly with wooden spoon until soft curds form. (The texture should be that of a loose, lumpy pudding.) Immediately transfer to four small ramekins. Top each with dollop of sour cream and 1 teaspoonful of caviar. Serve hot with toast or crackers.

SERVES 4

Anatomy of an Egg

An egg is the unhatched reproductive unit of a female chicken. It consists of a yolk and a white enclosed in a shell, with an air pocket at the wider end, and white threads called chalazae that bind the yolk to the white. Chalazae do not interfere with the culinary performance of egg whites, and though they may be removed, there is no need to do so. The fresher the egg, the more prominent the chalazae.

HOT EGG AND BACON SALAD

In this classic French bistro salad, also known as a Lyonnaise, the runny yolk from a delicately poached egg enriches a silky salad dressing.

¼ pound thickly sliced bacon, cut across width into ¼-inch strips
¼ cup white wine vinegar
4 eggs, cold
1 large head frisée lettuce, washed and broken into pieces
¼ cup red wine vinegar
1 tablespoon olive oil
salt and freshly ground pepper
2 tablespoons chopped fresh herbs such as chives, basil, *or* tarragon

Fry the bacon in a skillet over medium heat, stirring, until crisp. Transfer with slotted spoon to paper towels to drain. Reserve bacon drippings.

Meanwhile, fill a large skillet nearly to the rim with water and white wine vinegar. Bring to a simmer. Crack each egg and carefully drop, one at a time, into the water. Cook until whites are just set and yolks are runny, about 3 minutes. Transfer with slotted spoon to bowl.

Place lettuce in a bowl. Sprinkle the red wine vinegar, oil, bacon drippings, and fried bacon over salad. Toss well, and season with salt and pepper. Divide salad into four serving bowls. Top each with an egg, sprinkle with herbs, and serve warm.

SERVES 4

The Yolks

Egg yolks, or yellows, contain all of the egg's fat, about half of its protein, and three-quarters of its calories. An egg with a double yolk is probably the product of a young hen whose reproductive cycle has not yet stabilized. Yolks are great thickeners and enrichers, and, of course, they color foods yellow.

CRAB AND EGG DROP SOUP

The flavor and texture of crab and eggs mirror each other in this easy, elegant Chinese broth.

4 cups chicken broth
1 cup corn kernels, fresh *or* frozen
2 eggs, beaten
½ pound cooked crabmeat in chunks
1 teaspoon sesame oil
1 teaspoon rice wine vinegar
salt and freshly ground pepper

Bring the chicken broth to a boil in medium saucepan. Add corn, and cook over medium-high 2 minutes. Reduce heat to medium-low. Stir 1 tablespoon of hot broth into eggs in a bowl. Slowly drizzle the eggs into broth, stirring briskly to disperse into threads. Stir in crab and remaining ingredients, and serve hot.

SERVES 4

The Whites

Egg whites, also called albumen, are fat-free and high in protein. When beaten or whisked, they capture the air bubbles that make cakes and other confections rise. For maximum volume, separate eggs while cold and then let whites sit at room temperature 30 minutes or gently warm over low heat. Always beat in a perfectly clean bowl (preferably not plastic)—fats or oils will inhibit rising. With the whisk of an electric mixer, start beating at medium speed until foamy. Add cream of tartar or salt if using, and continue beating at high speed until peaks form. Be careful not to overbeat, since whites can turn brittle and break down. Use ⅛ teaspoon tartar per egg white; one white equals 1 liquid tablespoon. Unbeaten whites may be frozen.

GREEK EGG AND LEMON SOUP

This is a great dish to have in your repertoire for when the cupboard is relatively bare and the wind blows cold. Its Greek name is avgolemono.

5 cups chicken broth
½ cup long-grained rice
3 egg yolks
⅓ cup lemon juice
salt and freshly ground pepper

Bring the chicken broth to a boil in a medium saucepan. Stir in the rice, reduce heat to medium-low, and cook, uncovered, about 20 minutes.

Meanwhile, in a small bowl whisk the egg yolks until foamy. Slowly drizzle in lemon juice, whisking continuously. Ladle about 1 cup hot broth into egg mixture, whisking constantly. (Be careful not to bring to a boil.) Remove saucepan from heat, and stir in egg/broth mixture. Adjust salt and pepper to taste, and serve hot.

SERVES 4

Egg Safety

Outbreaks of Salmonella enteritidis, *a bacterial infection, have been traced to contaminated eggs. Though the likelihood of it occurring in any one egg is 1 in 20,000, the following precautions are recommended by the American Egg Board: Refrigerate raw and cooked eggs, discard eggs that arrive cracked in the carton, and thoroughly clean utensils after they've touched eggs. Unless eggs are thoroughly cooked, they still may be carriers. A temperature of 140 degrees F is high enough to kill bacteria.*

CHAWAN MUSHI

This traditional Japanese egg custard, taught to me by Los Angeles educator Diane Watanabe, makes a delicate first course or small, restorative lunch. A small chunk of cooked chicken, a ginkgo nut, a spinach leaf or two, or a baby shrimp would also be lovely hiding on the bottom.

4 dried shiitake mushrooms
1 teaspoon sugar
1 teaspoon soy sauce
½ cup boiling water
4 eggs
1½ cups chicken *or* fish stock

Place the mushrooms, sugar, and soy sauce in small bowl. Add boiling water, and soak 20 minutes to soften. Remove mushrooms, trim stems, and thickly slice caps. Reserve soaking liquid.

Lightly beat the eggs in a large mixing bowl. Stir in the chicken or fish stock and the mushroom-soaking liquid.

Place 1 sliced mushroom each on the bottom of four coffee cups or 8-ounce ramekins. Pour egg/chicken stock mixture into cups nearly to the top. Cover each cup lightly with foil. Place on rack in steamer. Cook over simmering water 20 to 25 minutes, just until set. Serve hot with spoons.

SERVES 4

The Nutritional Egg

The egg is considered one of the most nutritious foods on the planet. In one neat little package are all nine amino acids, more protein per serving than in beef or fish, and nearly every dietary vitamin and mineral except vitamin C. Eggs also contain a high ratio of cholesterol, the reason for their downward spiral in consumption during the last twenty years. The latest findings, however, indicate that dietary cholesterol does not necessarily raise blood cholesterol levels. So except for someone considered at high risk due to already elevated tri-glycerides and blood cholesterol, moderate egg consumption is now condoned by the American Heart Association. Stay tuned.

EGGS IN THE AFTERNOON

CAJUN SPICED EGGS

This easy casserole would be terrific for a New Orleans-style brunch with chicory coffee and beignets.

3 tablespoons olive oil
½ onion, chopped
2 garlic cloves, minced
¼ cup diced celery
¼ cup each diced red and green bell pepper
2 ounces honey-cured ham, diced
½ teaspoon paprika
¼ teaspoon cayenne
¼ teaspoon dried thyme
1½ cups canned crushed tomatoes
salt and freshly ground pepper
4 eggs
2 tablespoons chopped fresh Italian parsley

Heat the olive oil in a large skillet over medium-low heat. Cook the onion and garlic to soften, 5 minutes. Add celery, and red and green bell pepper, and cook until soft. Turn the heat up to medium-high, add ham, and cook 2 minutes. Stir in paprika, cayenne, and thyme, and cook less than 1 minute. Pour in tomatoes, season with salt and pepper, and simmer about 10 minutes to thicken.

Preheat oven to 400 degrees F.

Pour tomato sauce into 9-inch-square ceramic baking pan. One at a time, carefully break the eggs over the sauce, and sprinkle with parsley. Bake 18 to 20 minutes or until eggs are done to taste. Serve with warm, crusty bread for dipping.

SERVES 4

PIZZA AND EGGS

For more spice, top with tomato salsa, or for more savor, add crumbled cooked bacon under the eggs.

2 tablespoons olive oil
2 eggs, beaten
salt and freshly ground pepper
1 individual prepared pizza crust
1 cup shredded mozzarella cheese
¼ cup shredded cheddar cheese
1 tablespoon chopped fresh Italian
parsley

Heat 1 tablespoon oil in 8-inch skillet over high heat. Season the eggs with salt and pepper, and pour into pan. Swirl to coat bottom, and then reduce heat to low.

Cook until bottom is set and top is still liquid, about 2 minutes. Set aside.

Preheat oven to 450 degrees F.

Place pizza crust on baking sheet. Coat with remaining oil, and sprinkle with half the cheeses, leaving edges bare. Bake about 5 minutes, until cheese is melted. Remove from oven, and place unbroken eggs over cheese with spatula. Sprinkle with parsley, and top with remaining cheese. Return to oven and bake 5 minutes longer, until edges are brown.

MAKES 1

"Probably one of the most private things in the world is an egg until it is broken."

—*from* How to Cook a Wolf *by M.F.K. Fisher*

EGGS, ONIONS, AND LOX

This classic New York egg dish is a good way to stretch a little bit of luxurious smoked salmon. Bagels, bialys, or rye toast are the authentic accompaniments.

4 eggs
1 to 2 tablespoons cold water *or* milk
salt and freshly ground pepper
2 tablespoons butter
½ large onion, chopped
¼ pound thinly sliced lox, roughly
    chopped
sliced chives as garnish

In a small bowl, beat together eggs, water or milk, salt, and pepper. Set aside.

Melt the butter in a large nonstick skillet over medium heat. Add the onion, salt, and pepper, and cook until onion begins to brown. Add the lox, reduce heat to medium-low, and cook, stirring occasionally, until color turns beige. Pour in eggs, reduce heat, and cook, stirring constantly, just until eggs are loosely set. Sprinkle with chives, and serve hot.

SERVES 2

To tell whether an egg in the shell is cooked or not, hold it on a counter, pointy-end down, and spin. A raw egg will topple, while a cooked egg will spin like a top.

ASPARAGUS QUICHE

Quiche deserves a special place in the culinary firmament for dishes that may fall from favor but refuse to disappear.

1 unbaked pie *or* tart shell
1 pound asparagus, trimmed and cut in
   ½-inch lengths
1 tablespoon butter
2 shallots, diced
4 eggs
½ cup heavy cream
¾ cup grated Gruyère *or* Parmesan cheese
salt and freshly ground pepper

Preheat oven to 375 degrees F. Line pie shell with paper and weights, and bake 10 minutes. Remove weights and set aside.

Microwave the asparagus with 1 tablespoon of water for 2 minutes at full power. Drain.

Melt the butter in a medium skillet over medium heat. Sauté the shallots until soft. Add asparagus, and continue cooking 10 minutes.

In a large bowl, whisk together eggs, cream, ½ cup of the cheese, salt, and pepper. Add the asparagus, and mix to combine. Season with salt and pepper.

Pour into the prepared pie shell, sprinkle remaining cheese over top, and bake until golden brown and puffy, about 40 minutes. Cool 10 minutes, cut into wedges, and serve.

SERVES 6 TO 8

ZUCCHINI FRITTATA

Frittatas make a great weeknight family dinner with a salad and some crusty bread.

8 eggs
2 medium zucchini, trimmed and grated
4 ounces thinly sliced prosciutto, torn in shreds
1/4 cup grated Parmesan cheese
3 tablespoons chopped fresh Italian parsley
salt and freshly ground pepper
1 tablespoon olive oil

Beat the eggs in a large mixing bowl. Add zucchini, prosciutto, Parmesan, parsley, salt, and pepper. Mix to combine.

Preheat the broiler.

Heat the oil in a large ovenproof skillet, preferably nonstick or cast-iron, over medium-high heat. Pour in the egg mixture and swirl to set evenly. Smooth the top with a fork. Reduce the heat to medium-low, and cook, uncovered, until the edges are set and the center is runny. Place under the broiler briefly, just to set, 1 to 2 minutes. Set aside to cool in pan 5 minutes. Slide onto a platter to serve. Cut into wedges and serve warm or at room temperature.

SERVES 6 TO 8

HUEVOS RANCHEROS

*On my first trip to Mexico, I had some trouble
adjusting to the* caliente *breakfast foods that
I have come to love for lunch or dinner.*

vegetable oil for frying
4 corn tortillas
4 eggs
1½ cups prepared red salsa, warmed
2 tablespoons crumbled feta cheese
2 tablespoons chopped fresh cilantro
freshly ground pepper

Pour oil into a small skillet to a depth of ¼ inch. Fry tortillas one at a time over medium heat until barely crisp, about 1 minute per side. Drain on paper towels.

Spoon 2 tablespoons of the hot oil into a large skillet, preferably nonstick. Fry the eggs all at once, sunny-side up, until the whites are just set.

To serve, arrange 2 tortillas on each plate, so they overlap in the center. Top each tortilla with an egg. Spoon the warm salsa over the whites and tortillas. Sprinkle cheese and cilantro over all, and grind pepper over yolks. Serve hot.

SERVES 2

SCOTCH EGG

1 pound of your favorite sausage meat,
    cases removed
8 hard-boiled eggs, peeled and chilled
2 cups bread crumbs
vegetable oil for frying
3 eggs, beaten
tomato wedges for garnish

Divide sausage meat into 8 portions. One at a time, form a patty with meat, and flatten. Place hard-boiled egg inside, and keep rolling egg in meat until a thin layer of meat coats the egg. Chill ½ hour.

Arrange bread crumbs and eggs in two bowls. Dip each egg first in bread crumbs, then in eggs, and then in bread crumbs again. Transfer to refrigerator.

Preheat oven to 350 degrees F.

Pour oil into a large pot to a depth of 4 inches. Bring to deep-fry temperature of 350 degrees F. Fry eggs, 2 at a time, until golden brown. Drain on paper towels and then transfer to roasting pan. Bake about 10 minutes. Slice in half to serve with tomato wedges.

SERVES 4 TO 8

Free-range eggs are laid by hens who are raised outdoors. Oftentimes eggs laid by hens who are free to walk on a barn floor rather than in a cage are misidentified as "free range."

POTATO TORTILLA

The tortilla is the Spanish version of a frittata.
This simple one with potatoes, peppers, and
onion is exceptionally delicious.

½ cup olive oil
2 large baking potatoes, peeled and
    thinly sliced
salt and freshly ground pepper
2 garlic cloves, minced
1 large onion, thinly sliced
1 red pepper, roasted, seeded, and
    julienned
6 eggs

Heat ¼ cup of the oil in a 9-inch cast-iron
skillet over high heat. Fry the potatoes
with salt and pepper, turning occasionally,
until golden and crisp, about 15 minutes.
Drain on paper towels, and wipe pan
clean.

In another skillet, heat 2 tablespoons of the oil over medium-low heat. Sauté the garlic and onion until soft and golden. Remove from heat.

Preheat oven to 350 degrees F.

In a large bowl, beat the eggs. Stir in the cooked potatoes, red peppers, and the onion mixture. Heat the remaining oil in the potato skillet over low heat. Pour in the egg mixture, smoothing the top. Cook until the bottom is golden, then invert onto a plate. Slide the tortilla back into the pan, crisp-side up. Transfer to oven, and bake until the edges are set, about 5 minutes. Cool in the pan, and cut into wedges to serve.

SERVES 6 TO 12

WILD MUSHROOM OMELET

No dish engenders as much controversy in the world of egg cookery as the omelet. If another method works for you, by all means use it.

2 eggs
½ teaspoon sesame oil
salt and freshly ground pepper
1½ tablespoons butter
3 large shiitake mushroom caps, roughly chopped
3 scallions, finely chopped
½ teaspoon sliced fresh chives

In a bowl, beat together the eggs with sesame oil, salt, and pepper.

Melt 1 tablespoon of the butter in an 8-inch skillet over high heat. Sauté the mushrooms and scallions until vegetables are wilted and the pan is dry, about 2 minutes. Tip out into a bowl.

Return pan to high heat, and melt the remaining butter. Pour in the eggs, swirling the pan to coat evenly. Shake the pan, and lift the eggs with a fork. Scatter the reserved mushroom mixture over the center, and fold over to partially enclose. Continue cooking, shaking the pan frequently, less than 1 minute to set. Tilt onto plate, sprinkle with chives, and serve.

SERVES 1

Egg Grading

All eggs are graded A, AA, or B. There is almost no difference in quality between the A's—the type available at the market. B eggs, whose appearance may be less than perfect, are shipped to bakeries and factories that deal in broken-egg products such as frozen waffles and the like.

GREEK OMELET

This puffy omelet is a sort of cross between an Italian frittata and a French omelet. The mixture of earthy Greek flavors is a favorite of mine.

4 eggs
2 tablespoons water
Tabasco to taste
freshly ground pepper
1 tablespoon olive oil
4 scallions, trimmed and chopped
1 plum tomato, seeded and chopped
1 tablespoon chopped fresh mint
2 ounces feta cheese, crumbled

In a bowl, beat together eggs, water, Tabasco, and freshly ground pepper.

Heat the oil in a large nonstick skillet over high heat. Pour in the eggs, and cook over medium-high heat until edges just set. Sprinkle scallions, tomato, mint, and feta over eggs. Reduce heat to low, and cook until eggs are nearly set. Using two spatulas, flip over opposite sides to meet in center. Turn out onto platter and serve.

SERVES 2 TO 3

"As everyone knows, there is only one infallible recipe for the perfect omelet: your own."
> —*from* French Provincial Cooking
> *by Elizabeth David*

MATZO BREI

During the Jewish holiday of Passover, when bread is forbidden, matzo, a plain square cracker, takes its place. This is the matzo version of French toast.

6 matzos
boiling water
4 eggs, beaten
salt and freshly ground pepper
5 tablespoons butter
cinnamon sugar (optional)

Break the matzos into uneven pieces, about 1½ inches square, and place in a bowl. Pour boiling water over to cover and then immediately drain. The matzos should be wet but not soggy. Add matzos to bowl with beaten eggs. Season with salt and pepper, and toss to coat evenly.

Melt 3 tablespoons of the butter in a large skillet over medium-high heat. Add the matzo-egg mixture, and cook until bottom is browned. Then, with a spatula, turn in chunks, adding remaining butter to pan. Fry until edges are crisp and golden. Serve in craggy chunks, and sprinkle with cinnamon sugar if desired.

SERVES 3

A red blood spot on the yolk is a ruptured blood vessel. These spots are safe to eat and are not a sign of fertilization.

FAUX EGG NOODLES

From chefs Mary Sue Milliken and Susan Feniger I learned this unusual Peruvian dish—thin pancake omelets that are sliced into ribbons, or "noodles."

9 eggs
coarse salt and freshly ground pepper
¼ cup grated Parmesan cheese
¼ cup finely crushed water crackers
1 tablespoon butter, softened
2 cups prepared Italian tomato sauce for pasta, heated
¼ cup chopped fresh basil
grated Parmesan cheese

In a large mixing bowl, whisk together all the eggs, salt, and pepper. Add Parmesan and crackers, and whisk to combine.

Heat a large nonstick skillet over medium heat and lightly coat with butter. Ladle enough eggs into pan to form a thin layer. Cook until set, about 1 minute. Then slide onto a large plate, invert, and slide back into pan to set bottom. Cook less than 1 minute, and slide onto another plate. Continue cooking, stacking omelets, and adding butter to pan as needed. Cool slightly.

Stack 2 omelets at a time, and roll into a cylinder. Cut crosswise into ¼-inch-wide strips. Transfer egg strips to hot tomato sauce, and toss to heat through. Sprinkle with basil, and serve like pasta with Parmesan cheese.

SERVES 4 TO 6

HUEVOS MOTULENOS

The motuleno, a casserole with ham and beans, is a specialty of the southern state of Oaxaca in Mexico.

8 corn tortillas
corn or vegetable oil for frying
2 cups prepared Mexican ranchera sauce
   or tomato salsa
½ cup drained, canned black beans
3 ounces diced ham
½ cup grated Parmesan cheese
4 eggs

Preheat oven to 350 degrees F.

If fresh, let tortillas sit out 30 minutes to dry. Pour oil to a depth of ¼ inch in a small skillet, and place over medium-low heat. Fry the tortillas one at a time, just to soften on both sides, less than 1 minute total. Drain on paper towels. Carefully pour off all but about 1 tablespoon of oil from the pan.

Coat the bottom of a 9- or 10-inch-square ovenproof casserole with 1 cup of sauce. Top with a layer of 4 tortillas. Sprinkle with beans, ham, and ¼ cup of cheese. Top with another tortilla layer, and the remaining sauce and cheese. Bake about ½ hour.

Warm the tortilla skillet over medium heat. Fry the eggs sunny-side up two at a time, and place over warm casserole. Serve hot.

SERVES 4

"Once an egg is taken out of the breakfast category and put to use as a hot entrée, a luncheon, or a supper dish,...you can draw on practically your whole cooking experience for its saucing and garnishing."

—*from* Mastering the Art of French Cooking, Vol. I, *by Julia Child*

CHORIZO AND EGGS

Chorizo is a rich pork sausage from Mexico.

3 chorizos, casings removed
1 tablespoon vegetable oil
1 medium onion, diced
8 eggs, beaten
salt and freshly ground pepper
cilantro sprigs for garnish

Fry the chorizos in a medium skillet over medium-low heat, crumbling the meat with a spoon to brown evenly, about 5 minutes.

Push the meat to the edges of the pan, and warm the oil in the center. Cook the onion in oil about 5 minutes to soften, then stir together and cook sausage and onion, 4 minutes longer.

Season the eggs with salt and pepper. Pour into pan, reduce heat to low, and scramble along with the meat and onions until eggs are just done. Garnish with cilantro, and serve with warm tortillas.

SERVES 4

"...It might seem that an egg which has succeeded in being fresh has done all that can reasonably be expected of it."

—from A Little Tour of France by Henry James

SALAMI AND EGGS

This traditional Jewish favorite is full of spice and garlic from the flavorful salami.

1 tablespoon butter
4 thin hand-cut slices kosher salami, cut in quarters
2 eggs
1 *or* 2 tablespoons milk
salt, freshly ground pepper, and Tabasco

Melt the butter in a small skillet over low heat. Fry the salami until lightly browned on both sides.

Meanwhile beat together the eggs, milk, salt, pepper, and Tabasco. Pour into pan, and raise heat to medium. Cook, lifting edges and swirling pan to set evenly. When puffed and nearly done, flip with spatula to finish. Serve hot with toast.

MAKES 1

EGG BREADS AND BEVERAGES

EGG BREAD

To shape dough into the classic braids for Jewish challah, simply divide each portion into three parts, roll into strands, and braid, tucking the ends under to anchor.

1½ cups warm water
3 tablespoons sugar
2 (¼-ounce) packages dry yeast
6 to 6 ½ cups all-purpose flour
2 teaspoons coarse salt
⅓ cup vegetable shortening
3 eggs
1 egg yolk beaten with 1 tablespoon
    water, for glaze
poppy *or* sesame seeds for sprinkling
    (optional)

In a liquid measuring cup, stir together ½ cup of the water, the sugar, and yeast. Set aside to foam.

In the bowl of an electric mixer, place 4 cups of the flour, the salt, and the shortening. Mix with paddle at low speed to form crumbly mixture. Add the eggs, the yeast mixture, 2 additional cups flour, and the remaining 1 cup water. Mix to combine, and then switch to the dough hook.

Knead at low speed, sprinkling in remaining flour until dough is smooth and elastic, 5 to 10 minutes. Remove, and knead by hand on unfloured counter about 1 minute. Place in buttered bowl, turning to coat evenly, and cover with plastic wrap. Cover with towels, and let rise until doubled, 1 to 2 hours.

Punch down dough, divide in half, and lightly knead each into a ball. Let rest 10 minutes. Roll out each so the length fits a 9 x 5-inch loaf pan. Coat two loaf pans with butter or spray, and place dough inside. Cover, and let rest 45 minutes.

To bake, preheat oven to 375 degrees F. Brush loaves with egg glaze and sprinkle with seeds, if desired.

Bake about 45 minutes, until tops are golden and bread sounds hollow when tapped. Cool on racks.

MAKES 2 LOAVES

"Few employments are better suited to women of small capital, either of money or physical strength, than the raising of eggs for market."
—from Eggs *by Anna Burrows*

ULTIMATE FRENCH TOAST

After many years of making French toast for hungry kids, I find this simple version—preferably fried to a crisp—is my hands-down favorite.

2 eggs
3 tablespoons milk
⅛ teaspoon cinnamon
pinch of nutmeg
4 slices day-old egg bread
2 tablespoons butter
maple syrup *or* cinnamon sugar for serving

In a large shallow bowl, with a fork beat together eggs, milk, cinnamon, and nutmeg. Dip each bread slice on both sides in the egg mixture, and then let all slices soak for 2 to 5 minutes.

Melt butter in a large skillet over medium-high heat. Add the bread, reduce heat to medium-low, and cook until bottom is golden brown. Turn, and cook second side until done to taste. Serve hot with maple syrup or cinnamon sugar.

SERVES 2

CLASSIC EGGNOG

For those who want to take a walk on the wild side at holiday time—a classic uncooked nog.

6 very fresh eggs
1 cup confectioners' sugar
3 cups whole milk
2 tablespoons vanilla extract
½ to 1 cup rum (optional)
freshly grated nutmeg to taste

In an electric mixer, beat eggs and sugar at high speed until pale. Reduce speed to low. Add milk, vanilla, and rum, if desired, and beat until thoroughly combined. Chill about 8 hours. Serve garnished with nutmeg.

MAKES 1 QUART

"Organic eggs" are laid by chickens fed organic feeds.

TOTALLY SAFE EGGNOG

*Here is an updated eggnog, cooked like a cus-
tard, to calm the nerves of those who worry
about bacterial things.*

1 quart milk
6 eggs
½ cup sugar
1 tablespoon vanilla extract
¼ cup rum (optional)
freshly grated nutmeg to taste

Bring the milk to a boil in a heavy
saucepan. Remove from heat.

In a bowl, whisk together eggs and sugar
until pale. Stir in 1 cup of warm milk. Then
pour egg mixture into milk, and cook, stirring constantly, over low heat until thick
enough to coat a spoon, or 160 degrees F.
Remove from heat, stir in vanilla and rum,
if desired. Chill until serving time. Serve
garnished with nutmeg.

MAKES 1½ QUARTS

MOCHA FLIP

For those who like their alcohol disguised as a milk shake, cheers!

2 ice cubes
1 egg
1 tablespoon chocolate syrup
½ cup milk
4 tablespoons Kahlua *or* coffee liquer
ice cubes for serving

In a blender, process the ice to crush. Add egg, chocolate syrup, milk, and Kahlua or coffee liquer. Process until frothy, and pour into iced high-ball glasses.

MAKES 2

Chickens lay eggs until they are sitting upon a certain number. So if the eggs are continually removed, the (exhausted) hen will keep laying to fill the nest.

SWEET ENDINGS

ZABAGLIONE

This light, easy Italian dessert is lovely on a summer evening. Serve plain or topped with sweetened berries or softly whipped cream.

3 egg yolks
½ cup sugar
½ cup sweet marsala

In a bowl over simmering water or a double boiler, whisk together yolks and sugar until pale. Add marsala, 1 tablespoon at a time, whisking thoroughly between additions. Continue cooking over low heat, whisking constantly, until thick and creamy, about 10 minutes. Serve warm or chilled in wine glasses.

SERVES 4

STOVETOP LEMON CURD

Smooth, bright yellow lemon curd is delicious mounded into tart shells, spread between layers of cake, or simply spread on an elegant slice of pound cake. Homemade is infinitely more delicious than prepared lemon curd.

3 eggs
¾ cup sugar
¾ cup lemon juice
½ stick butter, softened

In a mixing bowl or top of double boiler, whisk eggs until smooth. Whisk in sugar and lemon juice. Place over a pot of boiling water or top of double boiler. Cook, stirring frequently, until thick and pale yellow, about 7 minutes. Remove, and stir in butter, a small piece at a time, until evenly blended. Cool, cover, and store in the refrigerator up to 5 days.

MAKES 1½ CUPS

POUND CAKE

No-frills cakes such as this one make a great deal of sense for the home baker. With its dense, moist crumb, it keeps well and is delicious served plain or topped with ice cream, berries, or lemon curd.

2 sticks butter, softened
1 cup sugar
1 tablespoon vanilla extract
¼ teaspoon ground nutmeg
5 eggs
1⅔ cups all-purpose flour

Preheat the oven to 325 degrees F. Line a 12 x 4½-inch pan with parchment or generously coat with butter.

In the bowl of an electric mixer at medium speed, cream together the butter, sugar, vanilla, and nutmeg until fluffy and white. Add the eggs one at a time, beating well and scraping down the bowl between additions. (If eggs curdle, switch to the whisk attachment and beat until eggs come together.) Sift the flour over the batter, and gently beat to combine. Spoon into pan, smoothing the top.

Bake about 1½ hours, until top is golden brown and a toothpick inserted in the center comes out clean. Invert to serve.

SERVES 10 TO 14

An eggshell's color is determined by the hen's color. Brown eggs come from red-feathered hens, white from white hens.

FLAN

A fabulous smooth-as-silk flan for pudding purists.

1¾ cups sugar
3 cups heavy cream
1 tablespoon vanilla extract
9 egg yolks

Place 1 cup of the sugar in a medium saucepan over medium heat. Cook, without stirring, until dark brown and fragrant, about 5 minutes. Quickly and carefully pour the warm caramel into eight 4-ounce ramekins. Tilt and swirl to coat bottoms and sides.

Preheat oven to 300 degrees F. Place the ramekins in a large roasting pan.

Bring the cream to a boil, stir in the vanilla, and remove from heat.

In a large mixing bowl, whisk together egg yolks and ¾ cup sugar until pale and thick. Whisk one quarter of the cream into eggs, and then pour in remaining cream, whisking constantly. Pour the custard into ramekins. Pour hot water into roasting pan, halfway up the cups' sides. Bake about 40 minutes, until centers are just wobbly. Chill. (Flan keeps about 1 week in the refrigerator.)

To serve, run a knife along inside edges to loosen. Invert onto serving plates, spooning on excess caramel.

SERVES 8

The flavor of eggs is so prized in Asian baked goods that extracts such as vanilla or lemon are seldom used, so that the flavor of egg can dominate.

OLD-FASHIONED NOODLE PUDDING

A traditional Jewish pudding, or kugel, *can be a rich side or a wholesome dessert.*

4 tablespoons butter, melted
¼ cup plus 1 tablespoon sugar
2 eggs, beaten
1 cup sour cream
1 cup creamy cottage cheese
¼ cup raisins
1 apple, cored, peeled, and thinly sliced
1 (7-ounce) package wide egg noodles, cooked and drained
1 cup cornflakes, crushed
1½ teaspoons cinnamon

Preheat oven to 350 degrees F. Coat an 8-inch-square pan with butter.

In a large mixing bowl, combine butter, ¼ cup of the sugar, eggs, sour cream, cottage cheese, raisins, and apple. Stir to combine. Add noodles and mix thoroughly. Pour into prepared pan, smoothing top.

In a bowl, toss together cornflakes, remaining sugar, and cinnamon. Sprinkle over top. Bake 45 to 55 minutes, until top is brown and crunchy and knife inserted in center comes out clean. Serve hot or cold as side dish or dessert.

SERVES 6

Fertile eggs, which can be incubated to hatch a chick, do not keep as well as regular eggs. There is no known nutritional advantage to fertilized eggs, but they do cost more.

SUNSHINE CAKE

If you get a kick, as I do, from watching eggs puff up a cake batter, this old-fashioned yellow cake, packed with eight eggs, will amaze. Serve plain or topped with lemon glaze.

8 eggs separated
¾ teaspoon lemon oil
½ teaspoon orange oil
1 cup sugar
¼ teaspoon salt
½ teaspoon cream of tartar
1¼ cups cake flour

Preheat oven to 325 degrees F.

In the bowl of an electric mixer, beat egg yolks with lemon and orange oils at medium speed until smooth. With machine on, slowly drizzle in ¾ cup of sugar until pale and thick.

In another clean bowl with whisk attachment, whisk egg whites at medium speed until frothy. Add salt and cream of tartar, turn speed to high, and continue whisking, drizzling in remaining ¼ cup sugar. Whites should be glossy with medium peaks when done.

With a rubber spatula, spoon one quarter of the whites into yolks, and gently fold. Add remaining whites, and fold until combined. Sift half the flour over batter. Gently and thoroughly fold. Sift remaining batter over top, and fold until flour disappears. Spoon into 10-inch round tube pan (nonstick if possible), and run a long, thin blade through the center to eliminate air.

Bake about 45 minutes, until top is golden and tester comes out clean. Invert tube over upside-down funnel on rack, and cool in pan at least 1½ hours. To release, run a blade between cake and pan, and invert.

MAKES 1 CAKE, SERVES 10

GRAND MARNIER SOUFFLÉ

Substitute your favorite sweet liqueur, such as Amaretto or Frangelico, in this light-as-air dessert soufflé.

butter and sugar for coating
4 egg yolks
2 tablespoons melted butter
3 tablespoons Grand Marnier
   or other liqueur
1 cup milk
½ cup sugar
2 tablespoons all-purpose flour
6 egg whites
pinch of salt
confectioners' sugar for dusting

Preheat the oven to 400 degrees F for 15 minutes, and position a rack in the lower oven. Lightly coat with butter and sprinkle with sugar a 2-quart soufflé mold.

In a large bowl, gently whisk together egg yolks, butter, and liqueur.

Combine ¾ cup of the milk and the sugar in a heavy saucepan. Bring to a boil.

Meanwhile mix together ¼ cup of milk with the flour. Pour into hot milk, reduce to a simmer, and cook, stirring, until thickened, about 3 minutes. Remove from heat. When cooled slightly, stir one quarter of the yolk mixture into milk. Then pour milk mixture into eggs. Stir to combine, and set aside.

Whisk the whites at medium speed until foamy. Add salt, and continue at high speed until stiff. Add whites to yolk mixture. Fold with rubber spatula to combine. Pour into prepared mold. Bake until golden brown, pouffed, and slightly wobbly in center, 20 to 25 minutes. Sprinkle with sugar, and serve immediately.

SERVES 6

COOKIES AND CREAM SUPREME

Since homemade ice cream is such a terrific children's party activity, I chose an appropriate add-in. Feel free to fold in fresh berries for more sophisticated tastes.

2 cups milk
4 egg yolks
½ cup sugar
1 teaspoon vanilla extract
1 cup heavy cream
5 chocolate sandwich cookies such as Oreos *or* chocolate wafers, roughly chopped in chunks

Bring the milk to a boil in a large saucepan. Remove from heat.

Combine the egg yolks and sugar in a mixing bowl, and beat at low speed until pale yellow. Pour ½ cup of warm milk into eggs, and whisk. Then pour all of the egg mixture into the milk. Cook over low heat, stirring constantly with a wooden spoon, until thick enough to coat a spoon. Remove from heat, and stir in vanilla. Stir in the heavy cream. Cool slightly. Transfer to clean bowl, cover with plastic, and chill at least 4 hours.

Pour cold mixture into ice cream maker and follow manufacturer's instructions.

When done, stir in the cookie chunks and transfer to a storage container. Store in the freezer 1 or 2 hours before serving.

SERVES 6

OPHELIA'S CELESTIAL EGG WHITES

Los Angles friend and graphic designer Ophelia Chong taught me this traditional light Chinese dessert. She also suggests garnishing each with a single berry, or using almond extract in place of the ginger.

3 egg whites
5 tablespoons water
5 teaspoons sugar
juice from ½-inch knob fresh ginger,
    grated *or* squeezed through garlic press

In a bowl, whisk together egg whites, water, sugar, and ginger juice until barely foamy. Spoon into four 4-ounce ramekins or teacups. Place on steamer rack, cover, and cook at gentlest simmer until set, 10 to 15 minutes. Serve hot or cold.

SERVES 4

"Egg dishes have a kind of elegance, a freshness, an allure, which sets them apart from any other kind of food, so that it becomes a great pleasure to be able to cook them properly and to serve them in just the right condition."

—from French Provincial Cooking by Elizabeth David

CONVERSIONS

LIQUID
1 Tbsp = 15 ml
½ cup = 4 fl oz = 125 ml
1 cup = 8 fl oz = 250 ml

DRY
¼ cup = 4 Tbsp = 2 oz = 60 g
1 cup = ½ pound = 8 oz = 250 g

FLOUR
½ cup = 60 g
1 cup = 4 oz = 125 g

TEMPERATURE
400° F = 200° C = gas mark 6
375° F = 190° C = gas mark 5
350° F = 175° C = gas mark 4

MISCELLANEOUS
2 Tbsp butter = 1 oz = 30 g
1 inch = 2.5 cm
all-purpose flour = plain flour
baking soda = bicarbonate of soda
brown sugar = demerara sugar
confectioners' sugar = icing sugar
heavy cream = double cream
molasses = black treacle
raisins = sultanas
rolled oats = oat flakes
semisweet chocolate = plain chocolate
sugar = caster sugar